THE PRACTICAL STRATEGIES SERIES
IN GIFTED EDUCATION

series editors
FRANCES A. KARNES & KRISTEN R. STEPHENS

Social & Emotional
Teaching Strategies

Stephanie A. Nugent

PRUFROCK PRESS, INC.

Printed in the United States of America.

ISBN 1-59363-021-2

At the time of this book's publication, all facts and figures cited are
the most current available. All telephone numbers, addresses, and
Web site URLs are accurate and active. All publications, organizations, Web sites, and other resources exist as described in the book,
and all have been verified. The authors and Prufrock Press, Inc.,
make no warranty or guarantee concerning the information and
materials given out by organizations or content found at Web sites,
and we are not responsible for any changes that occur after this book's
publication. If you find an error, please contact Prufrock Press, Inc.
We strongly recommend to parents, teachers, and other adults that
you monitor children's use of the Internet.

Prufrock Press, Inc.
P.O. Box 8813
Waco, Texas 76714-8813
(800) 998-2208
Fax (800) 240-0333
http://www.prufrock.com

Contents

Series Preface   1

Introduction: What is Social/Emotional Education?   3

Why is Social/Emotional Education Needed?   10

The Cognitive-Affective Connection   12

Social/Emotional Strategies for the Classroom
    Learning Environment   15

Social/Emotional Strategies for Groups   23

Social/Emotional Strategies for Individuals   28

Collaboration and Connection in the Affective Domain   31

Conclusion   34

Resources   36

    Social/Emotional Education: Books   36
    Social/Emotional Education: Web Sites   37
    Classroom Climate: Books   38
    Classroom Climate: Web Sites   39
    Group Strategies: Books   39
    Group Strategies: Web Sites   41
    Individual Strategies: Books   42
    Individual Strategies: Web Sites   43

References   45

The Practical Strategies Series in Gifted Education offers teachers, counselors, administrators, parents, and other interested parties with up-to-date instructional techniques and information on a variety of issues pertinent to the field of gifted education. Each guide addresses a focused topic and is written by scholars with authority on the issue. Several guides have been published. Among the titles are:

- *Acceleration Strategies for Teaching Gifted Learners*
- *Curriculum Compacting: An Easy Start to Differentiating for High-Potential Students*
- *Enrichment Opportunities for Gifted Learners*
- *Independent Study for Gifted Learners*
- *Motivating Gifted Students*
- *Questioning Strategies for Teaching the Gifted*
- *Social & Emotional Teaching Strategies*
- *Using Media & Technology With Gifted Learners*

For a current listing of available guides within the series, please contact Prufrock Press at (800) 998-2208 or visit http://www.prufrock.com.

Introduction: What is Social/Emotional Education?

While the cognitive domain encompasses the intellectual processes, the affective domain addresses emotional aspects. Krathwohl, Bloom, and Masia (1964) developed the Affective Taxonomy to provide criteria with which to classify educational objectives according to the depth, complexity, and thinking skills required. As addressed in the taxonomy, the affective domain involves the manner in which individuals deal with emotions, feelings, personal values, appreciation, enthusiasm, motivations, attitudes, and sensitivities to other people, things, or ideas. The Affective Taxonomy is comprised of five categories: receiving, responding, valuing, organizing, and characterizing.

Receiving

Receiving refers to the student's willingness to attend to various stimuli (class activities, textbook readings, etc.). Receiving occurs when the learner is aware or passively acknowledging material. From a teacher's viewpoint, it deals with getting, holding, and directing student attention. Learning outcomes at this level range from simple recognition that a topic exists to discerning attention by the learner. Objectives at this level may include such behaviors as listening, showing sensitivity, accepting differences, displaying tolerance, demonstrating awareness, or attending closely. Verbs frequently used for expressing outcomes at the receiving level include *ask*, *choose*, *describe*, *follow*, *identify*, *reply*, *select*, and *use*.

Responding

Responding relates to active participation on the part of the student. Responding occurs when the learner meets given expectations by attending or reacting to specific stimuli in the anticipated manner. At this level, the student reacts to the presented stimulus. From a teaching standpoint, this level concerns student interest in materials presented. Outcomes at the responding level may encompass acquiescence in responding (reading assigned material), willingness to respond (voluntarily reading beyond the given assignment), or satisfaction in responding (reading for pleasure or enjoyment). Instructional objectives in this category are typically associated with personal or academic interests. Objectives include behaviors such as following parameters, meeting expectations, participating, volunteering, showing interest, or enjoying. Verbs used to express learning outcomes at this level include *assist*, *greet*, *help*, *perform*, *present*, *select*, *engage in*, *spend leisure time in*, and *comply with*.

Valuing

Valuing focuses on the worth a student associates with the stimulus. Valuing takes place when a learner exhibits an external behavior that is consistent with a personal internal commitment when he or she is not forced to do so. This can range from a desire to improve group interaction skills to a commitment to a group project or assuming leadership responsibility in some aspect. Thus, valuing is based upon the internalization of a set of specified principles demonstrated by overt behaviors. Instructional objectives that are linked to attitudes and appreciation are found at this level. Objectives at the valuing level might include demonstrating a belief in, appreciating, showing concern, expressing a preference for, demonstrating commitment to, or exhibiting problem-solving behavior. Associated verbs include *complete, explain, form, initiate, invite, join, justify, propose, share, debate, support,* and *relinquish.*

Organization

Organization is comprised of bringing together different values and resolving conflicts. This is most often demonstrated by the identification and acceptance of one's own relative strengths and weaknesses. Learning outcomes at this level may take the form of conceptualizing a value such as recognizing the responsibility of each participant in a cooperative group for improving relations and communication or organizing a value system like developing a career plan that satisfies the student's need for economic benefit and social service. Instructional objectives that involve the construction and articulation of one's personal philosophy would be placed in this category. Objectives at this level would include recognizing the need for balance, incorporating planning in problem solving, accepting responsibility, or recognizing relative strengths and challenges. Verbs that could be used at this level include *adhere to, defend, synthesize, discuss, theorize, formulate, balance, examine, modify, integrate,* and *relate.*

Characterization

Characterization encompasses lifestyle and personal value system choices. At this stage, a student's behavior is pervasive, consistent, and predictable. Learning outcomes at this level cover a broad range of actions, but the student consistently acts upon and exhibits values that are congruent with his or her personal philosophy. Instructional objectives concerned with the student's personal, social, and emotional adjustment are appropriate at this level. Some objectives may include demonstrating self-reliance, practicing cooperation, showing objectivity in problem solving, or exhibiting self-discipline. Associated verbs may include *act*, *display*, *influence*, *qualify*, *question*, *solve*, *verify*, *serve*, *manage*, *resist*, and *resolve*.

Since emotions are not directly measurable, the criteria related to each of these categories focus upon the demonstrated presence or absence of an emotion or attitude as it guides or controls one's behavior. Figure 1 incorporates a teaching scenario based upon the "problem of pollution" within the Affective Taxonomy to illustrate the subtle progression through the five levels. The problem of pollution could be easily replaced by any other real-world problem-based learning topic.

Additionally, the levels of the Affective Taxonomy can be integrated easily into questioning strategies. For example, upon reading a story selection, the following questions could be incorporated in order to lead students through all levels of the taxonomy (Sisk, 1987):

- Did you anticipate the ending of the story? (Receiving–directing attention)

- What part of the story did you find most suspenseful? (Responding–behavior accompanied by feeling of satisfaction)

- What do you think is the moral of this story? (Valuing–ascribing worth or emotional acceptance)

- What was your initial reaction to the main character? How did your attitude change? (Organization–ordered relationship of complex values)

Taxonomy Level	Learning Outcomes	Problem of Pollution Teaching Scenario
Receiving	Awareness	As the teacher introduces pollution as a problem for society, the students first simply are aware of the words and concepts associated with the problem such as recycling, toxic, poison, waste, or renewable resources. At this point, they are neither "for" nor "against" pollution.
	Willingness to Receive	As the students become interested in the topic, they are willing to listen to discussions, watch video clips, and read material about pollution.
	Selected Attention	At this point, students are choosing to read about pollution at the exclusion of other reading choices they are offered. However, they still have not formed an opinion or taken a position on pollution.
Responding	Acquiescence in Responding	Here students begin to take on the position of their teacher. They have not yet asserted themselves to form their own individual opinions as a matter or personal convictions.
	Willingness to Respond	As the unit continues, a student may intimate that he or she is beginning to form his own position against pollution by voluntarily stating feelings to the class.
	Satisfaction in Response	Later, the student strengthens his or her position by defending it when necessary.
Valuing	Acceptance of a Value	At this level, the student has internalized his or her position against pollution.
	Preference for a Value	The student now accepts the need for managing the environment and begins to plan a solution for a local area of need.
	Commitment	At this point, the student has internalized this new viewpoint. His or her own beliefs will govern personal actions instead of the opinions of others.
Organ-ization	Conceptual-ization of a Value	Later, this student may seek to find connections among his or her stance on pollution and other areas of social or political concern.
	Organization of a Value System	This may result in organizing his or her personal views on a managed environment with his or views own such issues as civil rights and/or health care.
Character-ization	Generalization	Eventually, this student may become involved in a career centered around environmental issues.
	Internalization	And, within his or her personal life, he or she acts according to the beliefs he or she promotes during business hours.

Figure 1. The affective taxonomy in action

- If you were the main character of the story, what, if anything, would you have done differently? Why? (Characterization–generalization consistent with personal philosophy)

Such inquiries not only lead students through the entire affective domain, but they also parallel the cognitive taxonomy promoting higher order thinking.

Researchers interpret the components of the affective domain differently. Some elements associated with social/emotional education include:

- individualized value systems (Krathwohl, Bloom, & Masia, 1964);

- attitudes, beliefs, and values (Sellin & Birch, 1980);

- interests and appreciations (Carin & Sund, 1978);

- persistence, independence, and self-concept (Levey & Dolan, 1988);

- feelings, emotions, and awareness of self and others (Treffinger, Borgers, Render, & Hoffman, 1976);

- interpersonal relations (Treffinger et al., 1976);

- humanitarianism (Weinstein & Fantini, 1970);

- curiosity, risk taking, complexity, and imagination (Williams, 1970); and

- character and leadership (Delisle, 2001).

With so many factors linked to social/emotional education, the affective domain should be given a priority in school curricula.

However, prior to crises or overt threats, schools have traditionally paid little attention to the social and emotional needs of the student body (Peterson, 2003). Now, with such a strong emphasis being placed upon standardized testing and content standards accountability, the need to incorporate strategies aimed at addressing the affective domain is greater than ever.

Why is Social/Emotional Education Needed?

Numerous rationales have been cited as to why schools choose not to include social/emotional education within their curricula:

- the traditional lack of concern in education for the affective domain (Tannenbaum, 1983);

- attitudes on the part of adults that emotions are to be dealt with at home, rather than in the school (Elgersma, 1981);

- fear of indoctrination (Bloom, Hastings & Madaus, 1971);

- the position that, if the school meets the child's cognitive needs, social/emotional development will automatically follow (Mehrens & Lehman, 1987);

- lack of reliable and valid tools for assessing social/emotional functioning (Levey & Dolan, 1988);

- lack of clarity as to the optimal level of social/emotional functioning to be attained (Levey & Dolan, 1988); and

- the belief that healthy emotional development among students is automatic (Blackburn & Erikson, 1986).

However, these rationales do not diminish the fact that, when social/emotional issues are addressed and social/emotional needs met, students face their challenges with emotional balance and appropriate coping mechanisms that promote success in reaching personal potential (Roeper, 1995).

The Cognitive-Affective Connection

Williams (1969) recognized the need for the integration of both
the cognitive and affective domains in order to release creative
potential and increase motivation. William's Model for
Implementing Cognitive-Affective Behaviors in the Classroom
attempts to bridge those two domains through specific structured learning experiences that transcend factual information
and stress creative thinking in both the cognitive and the affective areas.

The underlying philosophies of this model include the
concept that learning does not take place in a vacuum. Rather,
many factors shape and influence the learning process, including students' emotions and feelings. Thus, the model operates
on a continuum of convergence and divergence, as well as the
cognitive and affective. Figure 2 lists the eight behaviors
Williams identified as part of the cognitive-affective continuum, their meanings, and examples of how they might be used
in the content area of art (Williams, 1970; Rogers, 1985).

Cognitive-Intellective		
Fluent Thinking	To think of the most . . . Generation of quantity; flow of thought; number of relevant responses; ability to generate a large number of answers to an open-ended question rapidly	What are the different kinds of textures you can find in this painting?
Flexible Thinking	To take different approaches . . . Variety of ideas; ability to shift categories; detours in direction of thought; ability to shift perspectives easily	Did the artist start with a black canvas and add white or with a white canvas and paint it black?
Original Thinking	To think in novel or unique ways . . . Unusual response, clever ideas; production away from the obvious; the ability to generate a unique product or thought	For what reasons do you think the artist tried to make this painting look like a photograph?
Elaborative Thinking	To add on to . . . Embellishing upon an idea; embroider upon a simple idea or response to make it more elegant; stretch or expand upon things or ideas	Some parts of this painting are very detailed an some parts are simplifications. What might account for the choices the artist made?
Affective-Feeling		
Curiosity	To have courage to . . . The capacity to be inquisitive and wonder; toy with an idea; be open to puzzling situations; ponder the mystery of things; follow a particular hunch just to see what will happen	Why didn't the artist have the subject dressed up a little more before he painted his portrait?
Risk Taking	To be challenged to . . . Willingness to expose oneself to failure or criticisms; take a guess; function under conditions devoid of structure; defend one's own ideas; the courage to take a guess and risk failure in a seemingly ambiguous setting	Pretend you are an archeologist in the 21st century who has come across this painting at your dig site. What will you be able to conclude from this painting about the culture of its century?
Complexity	To be willing to . . . The ability to seek many alternatives; see gaps between how things are and how they could be; bring order out of chaos; delve into intricate problems or ideas; the love of challenge and difficulty in ideas, problems, and solutions	Why did the artist paint so large a canvas of so ordinary a person?
Imagination	To have the power to . . . The power to visualize and build mental images; dream about things that have never happened; feel intuitively; reach beyond sensual real boundaries; the ability to use all of one's senses to generate images, ideas, and solutions	What could the subject be thinking? What kind of person do you think he is?

Figure 2. The Cognitive-Affective Continuum

Williams' model aids in defining affective behaviors that can be challenging to define. In addition, this model emphasizes open-ended learning environments and question techniques that lend themselves to both the affective and cognitive taxonomies (Maker & Nielson, 1995).

Once a comfortable classroom climate has been established, students are much more willing to share their own insights. An atmosphere of acceptance and personal responsibility, rather than fear of retribution or negativity, provides students with a safe haven where risk taking and personal reflection can take place. Research has shown that classrooms with open, democratic climates promote learning because such climates correlate significantly with the development of critical and creative thinking (Green, 2004).

Setting Parameters

One method for creating such an atmosphere within the classroom is the exploration and development of class parameters. Instead of dictating a set of rules and consequences to be used within the classroom, teachers can engage students in an open forum discussion about what kinds of behaviors promote their individual learning success and what types of behaviors undermine their learning.

Negative Statements	Positive Parameters
Do not criticize.	Provide positive, constructive feedback.
Do not speak out of turn.	Use respect and exercise good judgment.
Do not cheat.	Adhere to the school's academic honesty policy.
Lateness is not acceptable.	Show responsibility for your own learning by being prompt.

Figure 3. Transforming negative statements into positive parameters

Have students brainstorm a list of acceptable and unacceptable behaviors. Combine and restructure the brainstormed items into a positively stated set of classroom parameters (see Figure 3). Then, follow the same process to develop the consequences for not adhering to the established parameters. In so doing, students become stakeholders in the classroom community's parameters and consequences; therefore, there are no surprises, and responsibility of student behavior is based solely with the student.

Character Education

Teachers can help their students develop character not only through modeling positive character traits, but also through the integration of those traits in the content of the daily curriculum.

For example, try regrouping the selections presented in the literature text by character themes like tolerance, justice, equality, and honesty. For example, *What Do You Stand For? A Kids'*

Guide to Building Character (Lewis, 1997) has an ample selection of such themes with reproducible worksheets to help introduce and promote discussion in the classroom. Use each theme as a prereading activity by defining it, having students describe what such behavior looks like, and giving examples of that character trait in action through current events or daily activities. If the content area's scope and sequence is not flexible enough to allow the reordering of selections, then be sure that a positive character theme is unveiled in the discussion of each selection.

In subjects other than language arts, character themes can be identified in units being covered in social studies (e.g., justice, loyalty), science (e.g., ethics, integrity), and physical education (e.g., cooperation, fairness). Supplement the adopted text with current events stories or literature selections (fiction or nonfiction) that exemplify the chosen themes (see Figure 4). If such a task seems daunting, allow the students to do the research and find applicable current events stories or literature selections to expand upon the character theme.

Learning Styles

Being acquainted with students' learning styles will help teachers better adjust their own personal teaching style, as well as maintain a classroom climate that is inviting and comfortable. Figure 5 provides general teaching strategies and learning activity suggestions appropriate for each of the three basic learning styles. Have students complete a learning styles inventory to determine whether they prefer auditory, kinesthetic, or visual stimuli. Solomon and Felder (2004) provide an online version that is scored immediately (http://www.engr.ncsu.edu/learningstyles/ilsweb.html), as does the University of South Dakota (http://www.usd.edu/trio/tut/ts/style.html). Or, have your students take one of the many multiple intelligences (MI; Gardner, 1983) surveys to identify their relative strengths and weaknesses.

Content Area	Context	Character Theme	Current Event(s)	Literature Application
Social Studies	Development of the trans-continental railroad	Cooperation	European Union; agency cooperation in disaster situations	*The Procession* by Margaret Mahy; *Nicole's Boat* by Allen Morgan; *Lord of the Flies* by William Golding
Science	Experimental procedures	Ethics	Cloning; testing practices; corporate honesty	*Flowers for Algernon* by Daniel Keyes; *Mrs. Frisby and the Rats of NIMH* by Robert O'Brien; *The Wave* by Todd Strasser
Math	Check work and results	Respon-sibility	Native American land issues; reparations for Japanese-Americans placed in internment camps	*Where the Lilies Bloom* by Bill Cleaver; *The Mock Revolt* by Vera Cleaver
Foreign Language	Culture studies	Tolerance	Immigration policy; racial profiling	*Crow Boy* by Taro Yahima; *Summer of My German Soldier* by Bette Greene; *The Witch of Blackbird Pond* by Elizabeth George Speare
Physical Education	Rules for a game or sport	Fairness or Justice	Copyright infringement; stock trading practices	*To Kill a Mockingbird* by Harper Lee; *The Well: David's Story* by Mildred Taylor; *The House of Dies Drear* by Virginia Hamilton

Figure 4. Character theme integration

Learning Style	Traits	Strategies	Activities
Visual	Learn through seeing body language and facial expressions; Tend to prefer sitting at the front of the class to avoid visual obstructions, May think in pictures; Remember what they read and write	Use pictures, charts, and graphs; use highlighters; illustrate or use graphic organizers; incorporate multimedia; make written work as visually appealing as possible	Diagrams; graphs; photographs; posters; collages; games; newspapers, maps; charts; illustrations; displays; cartoons; hypermedia; presentations; puzzles; bulletin boards
Auditory	Learn by interpreting meaning through intonation, pitch, and rate of speech; Prefer lectures, discussions, oral problem solving, and listening to others' viewpoints	Rephrase points and questions; incorporate multimedia in the form of music, sound effects, etc.; read aloud; employ storytelling to emphasize important points	Oral reports; presentations; panel discussions; musical performance; debate; songs; verbal games; show and tell; peer tutoring; demonstrations
Kinesthetic	Learn through moving, doing and touching; Prefer a hands-on approach in order to explore the physical world around them; May need movement in order to focus; Possess motor memory-remembering how to do something after participating	Allow frequent breaks; encourage note-taking; encourage movement while learning new material; incorporate manipulatives	Surveys; demonstrations; body games; field trips; role play; interviews; charades/pantomime; blackboard activities; flash cards; labs; collections; learning circles; computers

Figure 5. Learning styles:
Traits, strategies, and activity suggestions

The Learning Disabilities Resource Community Web site (http://www.ldrc.ca/projects/miinventory/miinventory.php) provides an interactive MI inventory that generates an online report of dominant traits. The site also provides printable versions of the inventory in both English and Spanish. Figure 6 lists suggested learning activities suitable for integration into lessons to provide opportunities for learners in all of the intelligences to demonstrate their relative strengths in the classroom.

By attending to students' strengths and helping develop other areas, teachers accommodate more learners and give students a greater repertoire of product choices and problem-solving methods (Green, 2004).

Interest Inventories

By discovering students' interests, teachers can tailor curricula and projects to meet the individual needs of each student. Likewise, by doing so, teachers foster a community of caring and establish a positive repertoire that is not necessarily driven by the curriculum.

Develop your own interest inventory by asking students what they like to do after school, what sports they enjoy, what their favorite cartoon characters are, who is the most important person in their lives, what their favorite and least favorite school subjects are, and so forth. Use this information to tailor assignments, help students choose projects and research topics, write teacher-made test questions to increase tests' reading interest level, and develop classroom decorations pertinent to your students' interests.

Renzulli (1977) developed a commercially available interest inventory called the Interest-A-Lyzer, which uses open-ended questions to help students become more familiar with their interests and potential interests. For example, one item from the instrument presents the following scenario: *Pretend that someday you will be the famous author of a well-known book.*

Intelligence	Suggested Learning Activities
Verbal-Linguistic	Writers' workshop, journals, debating, storytelling, alphabetizing, literature circles, creative writing, class discussions
Logical-Mathematical	Predicting, Venn diagrams, surveys, research projects, sequencing, computers, experiment, outlining
Visual-Spatial	Illustrating, filmmaking, guided imagery, mind maps, map making, cartoons, murals, collages, graphing, graphic organizers
Bodily-Kinesthetic	Scavenger hunts, performing, building, crafts, experiments, simulations, manipulatives, computers, pantomime, role playing
Musical	Writing lyrics, cultural music, singing, musical games, drawing or writing to music, rhythmic patterns
Interpersonal	Interviewing, class discussions, problem solving, establishing group rules, group story writing, teaching others, sharing, cooperative activities
Intrapersonal	Journals, self-reflection, personalized contracts, autobiographies, setting goals, imagery, independent projects
Naturalist	Classifying, collecting, analysis, developing or seeking patterns, real-world applications, natures simulations and problem solving
Existential	Philosophy, global thinking techniques, self-reflections, meditation, guided imagery, service learning projects

Figure 6. Suggested learning activities for multiple intelligences

What type of book will it be (history, science, fiction, fashion, etc.) and what will the book be about? Students are then asked to create a title for their prospective book. Since the introduction of the original Interest–A–Lyzer, Renzulli has also created other specialized interest inventories (Renzulli, 1997), including a version for both primary and secondary students, as well as one specifically for adults. There are also instruments designed for gauging art interest for students in grades 4–12 and a separate instrument for primary students.

Most other commercially available interest inventories have a decidedly vocational or career-oriented bent, including the Campbell Interest and Skill Survey (Campbell, 2000) and the Strong Interest Inventory (Strong, 1994). These types of inventories are often used by school counselors to help students in career planning.

Addressing the affective domain within the context of the academic curriculum does not have to be an arduous task (Johnson, 2000). Strategies addressing the affective domain may be integrated into students' daily curriculum and activities. Such strategies may be used individually within content areas, or multiple strategies may be combined to form entire units focused upon a specific affective aspect (e.g., self-knowledge and exploration of giftedness). However, it should be noted that the success of many social/emotional strategies relies heavily upon the attitude, development, and comfort level of the teacher (Clark, 2002).

Bibliotherapy

Bibliotherapy is the use of literature to help understand and resolve personal issues (Frazier & McCannon, 1981). The interaction between the reader and the story through identification or universal experience, catharsis, and insight appeals to many gifted students (Nugent, 2000). Gifted students whose strengths lie in their ability to conceptualize and generalize often find success through bibliotherapeutic reading (Adderholt-Elliot & Eller, 1989). It is one of the most effective social/emotional strategies available to teachers, parents, counselors, and gifted students (Silverman, 1993).

After careful selection of a book or short story, develop activities and guided inquiry questions to aid students in the understanding and internalization of the book and the bibliotherapeutic process. Planning activities prior to the bibliotherapy session, like the sample provided in Figure 7, helps to ensure that guided discussion or structured activities take place. Short stories or novels used within the curriculum may also be used with bibliotherapeutic goals in mind depending upon the themes or issues presented within the context of the plot.

Cinematherapy

Like bibliotherapy, cinematherapy engages viewers in an interaction with the medium to examine specific issues. Using films that portray gifted characters, either major or minor, to address the social/emotional needs of gifted students has been the focus of several articles within the field of gifted education (Nugent & Shaunessy, 2003). Milne and Reis (2000), Hébert and Neumeister (2001), and Newton (1995) concur that teachers can effectively use films to help students understand themselves and cope with being gifted. Figure 8 provides a sample plan for using film clips in the classroom as a way to address specific social/emotional issues. When selecting film clips, teachers should identify which social/emotional characteristics are to be targeted during instruction. As with bibliotherapy, film clips from cinematic versions of short stories or novels used in the curriculum may be applicable to cinematherapeutic strategies.

Book: L'Engle, M. (1962). *A wrinkle in time*. New York: Dell.
Grade Level: upper elementary, junior high
Major Characters:
Meg Murray: An awkward, highly intelligent, but underachieving high school student who is insecure about her physical appearance and abilities and displays social immaturity, particularly not taking responsibility for her own actions.

Charles Wallace Murray: The extraordinarily intelligent 5-year-old brother of Meg who has a strong interpersonal connection with Meg and his mother. He exhibits uncanny empathy and entelechy. He hides his brilliance from most of society.

Calvin O'Keefe: A popular and athletic boy in Meg's high school. He is also very intelligent, but has never felt truly accepted for who he really is.

Mr. and Mrs. Murray: Both brilliant scientists (a physicist and an experimental biologist, respectively) who instill a thirst for learning and independence in their children.

Sandy and Dennys Murray: Meg and Charles Wallace's twin brothers, who are very athletic and popular in school.

Themes: *A Wrinkle in Time* is a classic retelling of the battle between good and evil and the ultimate triumph of love. Additional motifs are encountered through the life lessons Meg learns as she completes her quest to find her father. They include overcoming her desire for conformity and appreciating her own uniqueness; realizing and accepting that one person cannot know everything; and understanding the importance of communication even when words are inadequate.

Suggestions for Use in Bibliotherapy:
Understanding Giftedness: Charles Wallace realizes he is different. While he is intellectually gifted, he lacks the physical ability to do things like other boys in his class.

1. Have students define asynchronous development and give examples from their own life experiences when they have been touched by it.
2. Have students brainstorm the characteristics of an intellectually gifted child. Then, make a chart for each of the Murray children and Calvin O'Keefe and cite evidence from the book that indicates his or her giftedness.
3. Have students comment on the following quote from Charles Wallace: "I really must learn to read, expect I am afraid it will make it awfully hard for me in school next year if I know things. I think it will be much better if people go on thinking I'm not very bright. They won't hate me quite so much." Have they ever felt the way Charles Wallace does as evidenced by this quote? What coping skills do they use to combat it?

Ownership of the Gift: Meg, Charles Wallace, and Calvin all have issues dealing with conformity and others' expectations of themselves.

1. Have students discuss or journal about the pressures they face to be like everyone else. Then, discuss, brainstorm, or present coping skills that can be employed to combat such pressures.
2. Using collages, poetry, or some other form of personal expression, have students illustrate their unique abilities, the things that make them special.

Figure 7. Sample bibliotherapy guide

Film: Van Sant, G. (Director). (2000). *Finding Forrester* [Motion Picture]. United States: Columbia Pictures.
MPAA: PG-13 for brief strong language and some sexual references.

Major Characters:
* *Jamal Wallace (Rob Brown)*: An intellectually gifted African American high school student who prefers to hide his intellect in lieu of basketball with his friends in his New York City neighborhood.
* *William Forrester (Sean Connery)*: A famous writer-turned-recluse who befriends Jamal and helps him with his writing and self-discovery.

Summary: Jamal Wallace is an inner-city kid from the Bronx who has an aptness for basketball and a genius at writing. While always a C student, Jamal comes to the attention of a prestigious New York City prep school when he scores highly on his standardized tests. While Jamal is given a heavy load at his new school, both he and the school know that the real reason they took him on is for his prowess on the court. Befriended by a fellow student, Claire, and helped along by Pulitzer Prize-winning author and recluse, William Forrester, Jamal pursues his dreams both on and off the court while overcoming obstacles placed by his bitter literature teacher. As Jamal is shaped by Forrester, he finds that he is changing the old writer as well, forcing him to confront his past and his future.

Pertinent Scenes and Suggested Uses:
Conformity and Masking Talent: In the scene where Jamal's mother meets with his English teacher to discuss his standardized test results, there is a contrast between what the scores show and Jamal's behavior in school versus his behavior at home. He tends to hide his intellect in order to fit in with his friends, but he is a voracious reader and writer at home.
   1. Share through discussion or journaling instances when each student has hidden his or her gift in order to conform. Discuss the context of the conformity and alternate coping mechanisms that could be used in the future.
   2. Operationally define the term potential. Have students share through discussion, writing, or artistic creation what they feel their potential contribution to society is. Discussion goal-setting strategies to help students reach their potential.

Empathy and Challenge to Authority: After viewing the scenes where Jamal defends his fellow student during English class by correcting the English teacher's grammatical error and where Jamal engages in a quoting battle with the English teacher, discuss methods of teaching that are not effective with student in the class and analyze possible reasons for their ineffectiveness. Then, present or discuss coping skills that could be employed by students when faced with inappropriate teaching methods.

Stereotyping: After viewing the scene where Jamal is accused of cheating on his essay, discuss the role that stereotyping plays in prejudice. What is the root of prejudice? How can we combat it?

Figure 8. Sample film clip usage guide

Note. From "Using Film in Teacher Training: Viewing the Gifted Through Different Lenses," by S. Nugent & E. Shaunessy, 2003, *Roeper Review, 25*, pp. 128–134. Copyright ©2003 by The Roeper Institute. Reprinted with permission.

Arts Incorporation

Sometimes, no matter how inviting and nonthreatening a classroom environment is, some gifted students may not be comfortable with verbalizing their social/emotional needs. Others may not even be cognitively aware that they have social/emotional issues to address and are therefore at a loss when activities that require affective verbal disclosure arise.

Incorporating art into a content area activity is one method that can be used to access the affective domain of gifted students when verbal strategies are ineffective or as a companion to verbal activities. The use of collage is one strategy that allows students of all artistic skill levels to participate in a creative activity that may be used as an affective outlet.

For example, a discussion on the real versus the ideal has developed during a unit on justice. Using discarded magazines, you can ask students to create individual collages that depict what ought to be on one side and what is on the other. The pictures students choose to incorporate into their collages may reveal more about their perception of the real and the ideal than their discussion. Upon completion of the collages, allow students the opportunity to share their observations about their own work and the work of other students in the class. Debrief students on the applicable affective aspects of reconciling the real and the ideal, such as perfectionism, body image, and multipotentiality.

Developing metacognitive habits takes practice. Teachers who help students initiate, internalize, and strengthen such behaviors through direct instruction, modeling, and use of practice promote learning because the effective use of such strategies is one of the primary differences between more and less able learners (Green, 2004).

Self-Understanding

In order to reach their potential and move toward self-actualization, gifted students need to understand themselves and their abilities, both relative strengths and relative weaknesses. One way to begin the self-discovery process is to use a student questionnaire. Although many teachers use such questionnaires or inventories at the beginning of the school year to learn about their students and their interests, by using those instruments as a springboard for discussion, teachers can promote reflective and metacognitive behaviors, as well as identify coping strate-

Complete the following phrases to make true statements. Write your first instinctual response after reading the phrase.

1. I don't know why _____

2. If no one helps me _____

3. Some teachers _____

4. I hope I'll never _____

5. It makes me mad when _____

6. I'm happy when _____

7. Most people don't know _____

8. I'm tired of _____

9. I'm good at _____

10. I believe that _____

Figure 9. Open-ended response form

gies in use or in need of instruction. Have students complete several open-ended statements (see Figure 9).

Service Learning

One social/emotional characteristic that many gifted students share is a heightened emotional intensity and sensitivity toward societal and social problems (Clark, 2002). One way for students to address those feelings is to become proactive and "do something" about their chosen cause (e.g., homelessness, elder care, pollution).

Service learning is a way to incorporate such proactive measures into the curriculum. Service learning is a method whereby students learn and develop through active participation in thoughtfully organized service experiences that meet community needs while being integrated into the students' academic curriculum. It provides structured time for students to think, talk, or write about what they did and saw during the service activity and to use newly acquired skills and knowledge in authentic situations, thereby enhancing what they have learned in school and extending it beyond the classroom (Belbas, Gorak, & Shumer, 1993). The benefits of service learning extend well beyond the classroom to include the students, the school, and the community. Making a difference is a need for many gifted students, as they often bear the weight of the world on their shoulders by empathizing with the woes of our society and environment. Through service learning, they have the opportunity to help. And, because service learning activities are open-ended, gifted students are often excited by the possibilities and experience the full effect of their creativity.

Collaboration and Connection in the Affective Domain

When the affective domain is addressed within the classroom, the focus of instruction makes a fundamental shift from a teacher-centered to a learner-centered environment. When the teacher assumes the role of facilitating learning, rather than imparting knowledge, the construct of teaching as a *helping profession* is strengthened (Robertson, 2000). Although most teachers are not professionally trainer counselors, they find themselves assuming a "counseling" role on an almost daily basis. Teachers may not be prepared or equipped to deal with issues that may arise when dealing with the affective domain. Thus, it is essential that a collaborative support system be available in the form of school counselors, school psychologists, therapists, and special interest groups/agencies so that mental health issues can be appropriately handled.

The Surgeon General defined mental health as the successful performance of mental function, resulting in productive activities, fulfilling relationships with other people, and the ability to adapt to change and cope with adversity (U.S.

Department of Health and Human Services, 1999). From early childhood until late life, mental health is the springboard of thinking and communication skills, learning, emotional growth, resilience, and self-esteem. Often, when mental health is mentioned, thoughts immediately move toward the idea of mental illness, rather than mental wellness. However, students are inundated with messages about success—in school, in a profession, in relationships, in sports—without appreciating the fact that successful performance rests on a foundation of mental health (U.S. Department of Health and Human Services).

Collaboration among public health, mental health, and education agencies provides the opportunity to improve students' mental wellness within the context of social/emotional education (Association of State and Territorial Health Officials, 2002). Successful collaboration may include:

- shared use of school or neighborhood facilities, equipment, and resources;

- enhanced school safety;

- raising funds and pursuing grants;

- underwriting activities;

- acquiring nonprofessional volunteers and professionals, as well as others with special expertise to provide assistance, pro bono services, mentoring, and training;

- sharing and disseminating information;

- networking and providing mutual support;

- sharing responsibility for planning, implementation, and evaluation of programs and services;

- building and maintaining infrastructure;

- expanding opportunities for community service, internships, jobs, recreation, and enrichment;

- enhancing public relations;

- sharing celebrations; and

- building a sense of community (Taylor & Adelman, 2000).

Although such collaboration opportunities seem logical, administrative policies supporting collaboration must be in place at the school, community, and agency level in order for such collaboration to be successful.

On an individual level, teachers can educate themselves about the counseling and psychological services available to students through their districts. The school counselor can be a teacher's greatest resource while integrating the affective domain into the classroom. Additionally, teachers should become familiar with the mental health resources present within the community—not necessarily for referral purposes, but rather as sources of information, possible networking opportunities, and fertile grounds for developing speakers and presenters for various classroom topics and projects. Likewise, the Internet has a wealth of readily available information from professional organizations, special interest groups, and agencies with expertise in specific areas of need.

Conclusion

When students arrive at school for the first time and every day thereafter, they bring with them their collective experiences, both social/emotional and cognitive (Beane, 1990). More than just personal feelings and emotions, the affective domain encompasses preferences and choices that are tied to belief and value systems, aspirations, attitudes, and appreciations. Each of these aspects draws upon the combination of the cognitive and affective. Logically, such integration should be found in the school setting.

The social/emotional characteristics of gifted individuals, as well as the social/emotional needs related to those characteristics, have been well documented by researchers in the field of gifted education (Clark, 2002; Cohen & Frydenberg, 1996; Cross, 2003; Delisle, 1987; Roeper, 1995; Silverman, 1993). However, despite the evidence and support provided by the literature, proactive attention to the affective domain is still overlooked in many schools unless that attention is in reaction to some overt problem identified by teachers or the administration (Peterson, 2003). Addressing the affective domain within the curriculum is appropriate for all students, but it is essential for gifted students whose social/emotional traits may include divergent thinking, overexcitabilities, sensitivities, perceptiveness, and entelechy (Lovecky, 1992). Specific strategies to meet students' social/emotional needs can be integrated into any subject area through individual activities, lessons, curricular units, or separate units.

Resources

Social/Emotional Education: Books

Beane, J. (1990). *Affect in the curriculum: Toward democracy, dignity, and diversity.* New York: Teachers College Press.

This book outlines ways in which the subjects of morals, values, and citizenship can be reintroduced to students, detailing how this emphasis may contribute to a more humane future.

Blymire, L., Jones, C., Brunner, T., & Knauer, D. (1998). *Affective cognitive thinking: Strategies for the gifted.* Harrisburg, PA: Penns Valley.

This books is designed as an activities workbook for gifted students. It uses strategies based upon cognitive thinking theory and affective process skills. The workbook is photocopy-ready and contains specific activities for language arts, social studies, mathematics, and science.

Cohen, J. (Ed.). (1999). *Educating minds and hearts: Social emotional learning and the passage into adolescence.* New York: Teachers College Press.

With chapters detailing best practices in creating a positive school climate, social decision making and problem solving, emotional learning in middle school, conflict resolution, and tolerance, this book shows how several schools have been successful in implementing programs that effectively address the affective domain.

Kirschenbaum, H. (1995). *One hundred ways to enhance values and morality in schools and youth settings.* Needham Heights, MA: Allyn and Bacon.

This text provides easily adaptable activities that integrate aspects of the affective domain.

Social/Emotional Education: Web Sites

Kieve Affective Education Inc.
http://www.kieve.org

Started in 1926, as a summer camp in Maine, the Kieve Organization has grown to include summer camps for both boys and girls, an ocean discovery program, science and wilderness programs, and a leadership program. They offer a free e-mail newsletter that is packed with informative strategies and suggestions.

The Ethics Resource Center
http://www.ethics.org

The Ethics Resource Center (ERC) is a nonprofit, nonpartisan educational organization whose vision is a world where individuals and organizations act with integrity. This site provides information that can be used in classrooms to prompt ethical dilemma discussions.

Classroom Climate: Books

Canfield, J., & Wells, H. (1994). *One hundred ways to enhance self-concept in the classroom.* Needham Heights, MA: Allyn and Bacon.

This book offers more than 100 practical, class-tested exercises that can be integrated into the school day or used in specific self-esteem programs. The authors provide suggestions for organizing and sequencing the activities, which are based upon solid learning and psychological research.

Shoop, L., & Wright, D. (1999). *Classroom warm-ups: Activities that improve the climate for learning and discussion.* San Jose, CA: Resource Publications.

The easy-to-use activities in this book are quickly adaptable, easy to incorporate into a classroom, and, most of all, enjoyable to the students.

Freiberg, H. (1999). *School climate: Measuring, improving, and sustaining healthy learning environments.* New York: RoutledgeFalmer.

This book provides a framework for educators to look at school and classroom climates using both informal and formal measures. Each chapter focuses on a different aspect of climate and details techniques that may be used by classroom teachers to judge the health of their learning environment.

Classroom Climate: Web Sites

Tribes Learning Community
http://www.tribes.com

Tribes is an organization and a program dedicated to promoting caring, safe, and comfortable learning environments. This site provides information and suggested bibliographies, as well as staff-development opportunities regarding the Tribes program.

Group Strategies: Books

Gelb, M. (1998). *How to think like Leonardo da Vinci.* New York: Delacorte Press.

The author presents strategies for approaching challenges through problem solving, creative thinking, self-expression, aesthetic recognition, and goal setting.

McAuliffe, J., & Stoskin, L. (1993). *What color is Saturday?* Tucson, AZ: Zephyr Press.

Using analogies, this book encourages both cognitive and affective aspects of creativity. The strategies used in the book lend themselves well to arts incorporation in the curriculum.

Halsted, J. (1994). *Some of my best friends are books: Guiding gifted readers from pre-school to high school.* Scottsdate, AZ: Gifted Psychology Press.

Halsted provides background and research on the affective and cognitive needs of gifted students along with typical reading patterns of the gifted. Also included is an annotated bibliography of more than 300 books appropriate for gifted readers, indexed by topic.

Gold, J. (2002). *Read for your life: Literature as a life support system.* Allston, MA: Fitzhenry & Whiteside.

Offering a wide range of familiar books, the author illustrates the ways in which daily reading can lead to sound mental health and personal empowerment. It includes sections on reading for children and adolescents, as well as recommendations for reading in times of crisis, stress, and anxiety.

Odean, K. (1998). *Great books for boys.* New York: Ballantine.

This excellent resource for parents, teachers, and librarians has more than 600 titles that have been carefully selected and annotated and then organized by reader age and genre.

Odean, K. (1997). *Great books for girls.* New York: Ballantine.

This resource provides more than 600 titles selected to encourage, challenge, and nurture girls. Each book is annotated and provided with a reading level range by grade. The selected books are indexed by author, title, and category.

Stanley, J. (1999). *Reading to heal: How to use bibliotherapy to improve your life.* Boston: Element.

The first nonacademic book about bibliotherapy, this is an accessible, useful, and engaging tool that informs readers how to choose and use books for bibliotherapeutic processes.

Hesley, J., & Hesley, J. (2001). *Rent two films and let's talk in the morning: Using popular movies in psychotherapy* (2nd ed.). New York: Wiley.

This book provides concise descriptions of dozens of popular films and shows how they can be used to address specific issues (e.g., divorce, substance abuse, personal responsibility).

It also offers suggestions for selecting films and creating assignments.

Solomon, G. (2001). *Reel therapy: How movies inspire you to overcome life's problems.* New York: Lebhar-Friedman.

The author suggests film titles to address life's emotional problems. This book provides analyses of films to aid viewers in comprehending the film on deeper, more emotional levels.

Group Strategies: Web Sites

Americans for the Arts
http://www.artsusa.org

This advocacy organization provides information on how to increase the coverage of arts in education. The site provides a wealth of information to help justify arts incorporation, as well as links to local arts associations and agencies.

National Arts Council
http://www.nac.gov.sg

This site provides links and information on grants and innovative funding ideas for arts education.

Bibliotherapy Bookshelf
http://www.carnegielibrary.org/kids/booknook/bibliotherapy

A service of the Carnegie Library of Pittsburgh, PA, this site provides an extensive list of books categorized by issue. The site is updated frequently.

Cinematherapy.com
http://www.cinematherapy.com

This site, authored and hosted by Dr. Birgit Woltz, provides an index of films with suggestions for use as cinematherapy.

Individual Strategies: Books

Lewis, B. (1998). *The kid's guide to social action* (Rev. ed.). Minneapolis, MN: Free Spirit.

Beyond providing real-life vignettes of students who have made a difference, the author outlines the skills and steps needed in developing, enacting, monitoring, and evaluating social action projects.

Eyler, J., & Giles, D. (1999). *Where's the learning in service-learning?* San Francisco: Jossey-Bass.

This book explores service learning as a valid learning activity. The authors present data from two national research projects whose studies include a large national survey focused on attitudes and perceptions of learning, intensive student interviews before and after the service semester, and additional comprehensive interviews to explore student views of the service learning process. The book provides ideas for those interested in promoting service learning projects in their own settings.

Galbraith, J. (1999). *The gifted kids' survival guide: For ages 10 and under* (Rev. ed.). Minneapolis, MN: Free Spirit.

This book helps young gifted children construct their own understanding of what it means to be gifted. The book is filled with contributions from gifted kids providing insight and advice to other gifted kids.

Galbraith, J., & Delisle, J. (1996). *The gifted kids' survival guide: A teen handbook* (Rev. ed.). Minneapolis, MN: Free Spirit.

This book is filled with strategies, advice, and insights from gifted adolescents from all over the country. Arranged by issues, the book can help students understand themselves and their giftedness.

Kincher, J. (1995). *Psychology for kids*. Minneapolis, MN: Free Spirit.

This book provides 40 Personality Style Inventories (PSI) to help students learn about their own attitudes, opinions, beliefs, habits, choices, memories, ideas, feelings, and abilities. The PSIs are designed to help students understand themselves.

Kincher, J. (1995). *Psychology for kids II*. Minneapolis, MN: Free Spirit.

Volume II presents 40 experiments to help students learn about others' beliefs, attitudes, perceptions, differences, and styles of learning. The tests are presented in a student-friendly format and provide debriefing information, as well as resources for further information if students' interest is sparked.

Individual Strategies: Web Sites

The Strawberry Point School Service Learning Primer
http://www.goodcharacter.com/SERVICE/primer-1.html

This guide offers step-by-step instructions on how to create, implement, and assess service learning projects.

The Big Dummies Guide to Service Learning
http://www.fiu.edu/%7Etime4chg/Library/bigdummy.html

This easy-to-use site provides solid answers to common questions about service learning. The topics are categorized into faculty concerns, program concerns, student issues, administrative concerns, and nonprofit issues.

Learn and Serve
http://www.learnandserve.org

A comprehensive information system that focuses on all dimensions of service learning, covering kindergarten through higher education, school-based and community based initiatives.

Adderholt-Elliot, M., & Eller, S. (1989). Counseling students who are gifted through bibliotherapy. *Teaching Exceptional Children, 22*(1), 26–31.

Association of State and Territorial Health Officials. (2002). Moving towards a multi-system approach for child and adolescent mental health. *Mental Health Resource Guide.* Retrieved on April 23, 2004, from http://www.astho.org

Beane, J. (1990). *Affect in the curriculum: Toward democracy, dignity, and diversity.* New York: Teacher's College Press.

Belbas, B., Gorak, K., & Shumer, R. (1993). *Commonly used definitions of service-learning: A discussion piece.* Retrieved on December 1, 1998, from http://www.nicsl.coled.umn.edu/res/mono/def.htm

Blackburn, C., & Erikson, D. (1986). Predictable crises of the gifted student. *Journal of Counseling and Development, 64*(9), 552–554.

Bloom, B., Hastings, J., & Madaus, G. (1971). *Handbook of formative and summative evaluation.* New York: McGraw-Hill.

Campbell, D. (2000). *Campbell interest and skill survey.* Minneapolis, MN: NCS Pearson.

Carin, A., & Sund, L. (1978). *Creative questioning: Sensitive listening techniques: A self-concept approach.* Columbus, OH: Merrill.

Clark, B. (2002). *Growing up gifted* (6th ed.). Upper Saddle River, NJ: Merrill/Prentice Hall.

Cohen, L., & Frydenberg, E. (1996). *Coping for capable kids.* Waco, TX: Prufrock Press.

Cross, T. (2003). *On the social and emotional lives of gifted children: Issues and factors in their psychological development* (2nd ed.). Waco, TX: Prufrock Press.

Delisle, J. (1987). *Gifted kids speak out.* Minneapolis, MN: Free Spirit.

Delisle, J. (2001). Affective education and character development: Understanding self and serving others through instructional adaptations. In F. A. Karnes & S. M. Bean (Eds.), *Methods and materials for teaching the gifted* (pp. 471–494). Waco, TX: Prufrock Press.

Elgersma, R. (1981). Providing for affective growth in gifted education. *Roeper Review, 3*(4), 6–8.

Frazier, M., & McCannon, C. (1981). Using bibliotherapy with gifted children. *Gifted Child Quarterly, 25*, 81–85.

Gardner, H. (1983). *Frames of mind: The theory of multiple intelligences.* New York: BasicBooks.

Green, N. (2004). Classroom strategies that support student success. Retrieved January 1, 2004, from http://www.learn-live.nrw.de/angebote/greenline/downloads/class_strat.pdf

Hébert, T., & Neumeister, K. (2001). Guided viewing of film: A strategy for counseling gifted teenagers. *Journal of Secondary Gifted Education, 12*, 224–227.

Johnson, K. (2000). Affective component in the education of the gifted. *Gifted Child Today, 23*(4), 36–41.

Krathwohl, D., Bloom, B., & Masia, B. (1964). *Taxonomy of educational objectives: The classification of educational goals. Handbook II: Affective domain.* New York: McKay.

Lewis, B. (1997). *What do you stand for? A kids' guide to building character.* Minneapolis, MN: Free Spirit.

Levey, S., & Dolan, J. (1988). Addressing specific learning abilities in gifted students. *Gifted Child Today, 11*(3), 10–11.

Lovecky, D. (1992). Exploring social and emotional aspects of giftedness in children. *Roeper Review, 15,* 18–25.

Maker, C. J., & Nielson, A. (1995). *Teaching models in education of the gifted* (2nd ed.). Austin, TX: PRO-ED.

Mehrens, W., & Lehman, I. (1987). *Using standardized tests in education.* New York: Longman.

Milne, H., & Reis, S. (2000). Using videotherapy to address the social and emotional needs of gifted students. *Gifted Child Today, 23*(1), 24–29.

Newton, A. (1995). Silver screens and silver linings: Using theater to explore feelings and issues. *Gifted Child Today, 18*(2), 14–19, 43.

Nugent, S. (2000). Perfectionism: Its manifestations and classroom-based interventions. *Journal of Secondary Gifted Education, 11,* 215–221.

Nugent, S., & Shaunessy, E. (2003). Using film in teacher training: Viewing the gifted through different lenses. *Roeper Review, 25,* 128–134.

Peterson, J. (2003). An argument for proactive attention to affective concerns of gifted adolescents. *Journal of Secondary Gifted Education, 14,* 62–70.

Renzulli, J. (1977). *The interest-a-lyzer.* Mansfield Center, CT: Creative Learning Press.

Renzulli, J. S. (1997). *Interest-a-lyzer family of instruments: A manual for teachers.* Mansfield Center, CT: Creative Learning Press.

Robertson, D. (2000). Enriching the scholarship of teaching: Determining appropriate cross-professional applications among teaching, counseling, and psychotherapy. *Innovative Higher Education, 25*(2), 111–125.

Roeper, A. (1995). How the gifted cope with their emotions. In R. Medeiros (Ed.), *Annemarie Roeper: Selected writings and speeches* (pp. 74–84). Minneapolis, MN: Free Spirit.

Rogers, K. (1985). The museum and the gifted child. *Roeper Review, 7,* 237–239.

Sellin, D., & Birch, J. (1980). *Psychoeducational development of gifted and talented learners.* Rockwell, MD: Aspen.

Silverman, L. (Ed.). (1993). *Counseling the gifted.* Denver: Love.

Sisk, D. (1987). *Creative teaching of the gifted.* New York: McGraw-Hill.

Solomon, B., & Felder, R. (2004). *Index of learning styles questionnaire.* Retrieved January 1, 2004, from http://www.engr.ncsu.edu/learningstyles/ilsweb.html

Strong, E. (1994). *Strong interest inventory.* Palo Alto, CA: Consulting Psychologists Press.

Tannenbaum, A. (1983). *Gifted children: Psychological and educational perspectives.* New York: Macmillan.

Taylor, L., & Adelman, H. (2000). Connecting schools, families, and communities. *Professional School Counseling, 3,* 298–307.

Treffinger, D., Borgers, S., Render, G., & Hoffman, R. (1976). Encouraging affective development: A compendium of techniques. *Gifted Child Quarterly, 20,* 47–65.

U.S. Department of Health & Human Services. (1999). *Mental health: A report of the Surgeon General-Executive summary.* Rockville, MD: U.S. Department of Health & Human Services, Substance Abuse & Mental Health Services Administration, Center for Mental Health Services, National Institutes of Health, National Institute of Mental Health.

Weinstein, G., & Fantini, M. (1970). *Toward humanistic education: A curriculum of affect.* New York: Praeger.

Williams, F. (1969). Models for encouraging creativity in the classroom by integrating cognitive-affective behavior. *Educational Technology, 9*(12), 7–13.

Williams, F. (1970). *Classroom ideas for encouraging thinking and feeling* (2nd ed.). Buffalo, NY: D.O.K.

Stephanie A. Nugent is an assistant professor of secondary education at the University of Arizona South. She has authored and coauthored several journal articles and presented at state, regional, national, and international conferences on various topics related to gifted education. With more than 10 years of experience teaching in junior high and high school classrooms, her research interests include moral development, integrating the affective domain in secondary curricula, effective technology integration strategies, and developing teacher leaders. Dr. Nugent earned her Ph.D. in curriculum, instruction, and special education with an emphasis in gifted studies at The University of Southern Mississippi.